The Rent Day. a Domestic Drama

Douglas William Jerrold

[Second Edition.]

THE RENT DAY.

A DOMESTIC DRAMA,

IN

TWO ACTS.

AS PERFORMED AT THE THEATRE ROYAL DRURY
LANE.

BY DOUGLAS JERROLD;

AUTHOR OF

"THE BRIDE OF LUDGATE;" "BLACK EYED SUSAN;" ETC. ETC.

Malone
B. 308

LONDON:

PRINTED FOR C. CHAPPLE, THE KING'S APPOINTED BOOK-
SELLER, ROYAL LIBRARY, PALL MALL.

———

MDCCCXXXII.
PRICE THREE SHILLINGS.

TO

DAVID WILKIE, ESQ., R.A.,

𝕮𝖍𝖎𝖘 𝕯𝖗𝖆𝖒𝖆

IS

RESPECTFULLY INSCRIBED

BY

HIS OBLIGED SERVANT,

THE AUTHOR.

v

𝔄𝔡𝔡𝔯𝔢𝔰𝔰.

TO THE PERFORMERS.

To Mr. WALLACK the Author of "THE RENT DAY" owes many obligations. Under his friendly auspices the drama was introduced to the theatre. Under his tasteful direction, exercised in the various minutiæ of the scene, it received a value and importance which eminently contributed to its success. The public look only to the event; but the Author must be fully alive to the masterly skill, which, in the scenic preparation of his work, elicits points of illustration, and, fully entering into the meaning of the writer, reduces his theory to the happiest practical results. For this rare service, the Author is indebted to Mr. WALLACK; who, in the production of "THE RENT DAY," proved, had proof been wanting, that he was no less artist than actor. On this point the Author can speak under the sanction of the highest authority—no less than that of the great Painter, from whose triumphs of art the idea of the present drama originated. Throughout the piece, the taste of Mr. WALLACK enriched and gave effect to the general design. It is less requisite for the Author to advert to the acting of the representative of *Martin Heywood;* inasmuch, as the public continue to acknowledge in it, pathos, sensibility, and manly power; blended with a frankness, a homeliness of manner, presenting a dramatic combination of singular effect and beauty.

"THE RENT DAY" has indeed been fortunate, not only in the number, but in the quality of the actors, whose abilities have been displayed in it; combining, as it has, the truly feminine tenderness of Miss PHILLIPS—the quaint "simplicities," as *Sir Hugh* would say, of Mrs. HUMBY—the honest, hearty bluntness of Mr. Cooper, as *Toby Heywood*—and the humorous apathy of Mr. Harley, as the hero of the day-book and ledger, *Bullfrog*. Most worthy of these is the subtle, Tyburn coxcombry of Mr. H. Wallack's *Silver Jack*. The *Hyssop* of Mr. Bedford would demand an ode from "the Orpheus of highwaymen," to sing its villanous merits. Mr. Younge, in a part of some difficulty, played with considerable power and judgment, and did good service to the Author; who, in fine, holds himself a debtor *to all*, without exception, engaged in the representation of " The Rent Day."

Little Chelsea, Feb. 20, 1832.

DRAMATIS PERSONÆ.

——o——

	DRURY LANE.
Grantley	Mr. Brindal
Old Crumbs	Mr. Younge
Martin Heywood	Mr. Wallack
Toby Heywood	Mr. Cooper
Bullfrog	Mr. Harley
Silver Jack	Mr. H. Wallack
Hyssop	Mr. Bedford
Beanstalk	Mr. Hughes
Stephen	Mr. Salter
Second Farmer	Mr. C. Jones
Burly	Mr. Hatton
Sailor	Mr. Heaton
Rachel Heywood	Miss Phillips
Polly Briggs	Mrs. Humby

Tenants, Children, Villagers, &c. &c.

This Drama was first represented Jan. 25, 1832.

CONDITIONS AND REGULATIONS

OF

C. CHAPPLE'S

ROYAL ENGLISH CIRCULATING LIBRARY, 59, PALL MALL,

Which must be strictly adhered to by all Readers.

I. Subscribers paying £5 5s. per year, £3. 13s. 6d. per half-year, or £2. 2s., per quarter, will be entitled to the new Publications immediately on their appearance, and are not confined to any number of volumes.

II. Subscribers paying £4 4s per year, £2. 12s. 6d. per half-year, £1. 11s. 6d. per quarter, or 15s. per month, will be entitled to two volumes 4to., or four volumes 8vo., or six volumes 12mo.; together with Plays, Pamphlets, and Periodicals.

III. Subscribers paying £3. 3s. per year, £1. 16s. per half-year, £1. 1s. per quarter, or 9s. per month, will be entitled to one volume 4to., or two volumes 8vo., or three volumes 12mo.; and any new Play or Periodical Publication.

   ⁎ Subscribers, resident in the country, on paying, *in either of the foregoing classes*, one third more than Town Subscription, will be entitled to an extra number of volumes. And, for their accommodation, the Proprietor will provide boxes, which, together with the expences of conveyance to and from the Library, postages, &c. are to be paid for by the Subscriber.

IV. Subscribers paying £2. 2s. per year, £1. 8s. per half-year, 15s. per quarter, or 6s. per month, will be entitled to one volume 8vo., or two volumes 12mo.; as likewise the new Plays.⁎

V The Subscription money, *in all cases*, to be paid in advance, at the time of subscribing, and at the commencement of every subsequent term. Should the book or books, in the possession of the Subscriber, not be returned at the expiration of the subscription, it will be deemed a renewal of the period already subscribed for; the Subscription will continue open, and must be paid, till such books are returned; and they will be charged accordingly, whether read or not.

VI. Subscribers to give their names and residence, and deposit the value of the books which they take away. To change once a day, *but not oftener*, unless they choose to pay for the hire of the extra volume or volumes requested.

VII. No Subscriber to keep any new book, in 12mo. or 8vo., longer than two days, or in 4to. beyond a week; nor any other book beyond a month; on condition of keeping and paying for the same, at the price affixed in the Catalogue. Pamphlets, Magazines, or Reviews, must be returned in two days at farthest.

VIII. Subscribers lending a book or books to Non-subscribers, to forfeit their Subscription money; neither is it allowable to transfer books to other Subscribers. If any book is written in, torn, or otherwise damaged or defaced, either in the blank or printed parts, while in the custody of a Subscriber, that book, or set of books, (if it belong to a set) to be paid for at the price affixed in the Catalogue.

   ⁎ The very great injury caused by readers scribbling their remarks, and otherwise wilfully damaging even the most valuable works, has determined the Proprietor most strictly to enforce this rule.

IX. Non-subscribers to deposit the value of the work, and to pay for each volume, not exceeding in value 4s., *fourpence*; 7s., *sixpence*; 10s., *eightpence*; 12s., *ninepence*; 15s., *tenpence*; 20s., *one shilling*; 30s., *eighteenpence*; 40s., *two shillings*; and so on at the rate of *one shilling in the pound*—New books will be charged extra. Time allowed for new works: 12mo. two days, 8vo. three days; and 4to. one week. Should any book be detained beyond the limited time, it must be paid for in a rateable proportion.

   †‡† Attendance is given at the Library from Nine in the morning until Eight in the Evening; and no Library book can be delivered or received but within those hours.

   ⁎ This Subscription taken only for Town.

ADDRESS TO THE PUBLIC.

C. CHAPPLE offers his present Terms of Subscription and Conditions to the Public, in hopes of meeting general approbation; and begs leave to observe, that if his Catalogue be not remarkably *extensive*, it is, at least, *select*, and that every book enumerated, has actual existence in his Library.

A *voluminous* catalogue, in general, has more of *show* than *real* use; consisting, principally, of obsolete reading, and volumes seldom or ever called for.

The BIOGRAPHER will find the LIVES and MEMOIRS of all such eminent personages (both foreign and domestic) as have distinguished themselves, and have been rendered, by their talents, virtue, exploits, or singularities, objects of public notice and attention.

The HISTORIAN and GEOGRAPHER will here have access to a collection of interesting information and pleasing entertainment, arising from the new source which has been laid open within these few years, by the late voyages and travels, (illustrated with suitable maps,) which have been performed under the patronage, not only of our own government and commercial companies, but those of France, Russia, Holland, America, &c. together with those undertaken by private individuals, for the improvement and extension of commerce, and the advancement of genuine science.

The MISCELLANEOUS READER will meet with a general selection of *every subject* worthy attention, on the score of *instruction* and *information;* including a copious collection of NOVELS, ROMANCES, POETRY, and PLAYS, as well as various works on the MODERN SYSTEM OF EDUCATION, both *original* and *translated*. In a word, no means will be left untried, no expence spared, to render his Circulating Library a Choice Collection of instruction and entertainment.

It is presumed, the Terms of Subscription will be found *moderate;* particularly when the present unprecedented high price of books is considered, and the great expence necessarily and *daily* incurred, in procuring every recent and approved publication of merit in the various branches of literature.

In this undertaking, the Proprietor has endeavoured to establish a plan for the well supplying of his Subscribers with every new work, immediately on its publication; and he will always be careful to procure such a number of each, as will prevent, as much as possible, any disappointment or delay. He embraces the present opportunity of returning his most grateful acknowledgments to his Subscribers, and the Public, for the kind patronage with which they have hitherto honoured him; and he hopes that the strictest punctuality and attention on his part will insure him the future favours of his Friends and Customers.

C. CHAPPLE particularly requests his Readers will favour him with an early return of all NEW publications, in order to promote an immediate circulation. A strict compliance with this injunction, cannot fail to insure general accommodation.

To prevent disappointment, a list of TEN or TWELVE numbers, selected from the Catalogue, should be always sent with returned Volumes.

⁎⁎⁎ The price of the Catalogue is Half-a-Crown in Boards.

C. CHAPPLE being desirous of rendering his Library quite deserving of public approbation, most respectfully assures those Ladies and Gentlemen who may honour him with their names as Subscribers, that every attention will be given to their commands. A well selected collection of recent publications of merit, as also of all established works, in various fancy bindings, both elegant and tasteful, are always in readiness for purchasers, as also every article of Stationery of superior qualities.

THE RENT DAY.

ACT THE FIRST.

Scene First: An Apartment in Grantley Hall. Disco-
vered, Crumbs (the Steward), Beanstalk, Farmers,
their Wives and Children, Servants, &c. The Charac-
ters and Stage so arranged as to form, on the rising
of the Curtain, a representation of Wilkie's Picture of
*"*Rent Day*."*

CRUMBS. By my heart! there's nought so pleasant as
a rent-day.

BEAN. Thee be'st right, master Crumbs; nought;—
when the corn's in the barn, and the money in the bag;
but rent-day, wi' bad crops and low pockets, be an awful
thing.

1st FARMER. It be, indeed. See what it ha' brought
Phil Jones to. That seizure, master Crumbs, ha' broke
his heart. Warn't you a bit hasty like?

CRUMBS. Ha, friends! it's a sad task to be steward!
I often seize with tears in my eyes. What then? we must

B

keep a clear book. I never turn out a family but—*(to one of the farmers.)*—you don't drink your ale, master Stoke—with the greatest reluctance. Last week, when Miles and his children went to the work-house, it—*(to another farmer.)*—help your dame to some pie—it made me really uneasy. Yet one's feelings must suffer. One must keep a clear book.

BEAN. Where be Martin Heywood, I wonder? Ha! things ha' ne'er gone right since the old man died of a sudden. I had hopes to see Martin here.

CRUMBS. I've had hopes some time past. But here's a toast: *(fills a glass.)* here's punctuality to all tenants. *(they drink,—looking significantly at each other.)*

BEAN. Come, I'll gi' thee another. Here be mercy and liberality to all landlords!

ALL—*except Crumbs.* Well said. Mercy to all land-lords! *(drinking.)*

BEAN. *(to Crumbs.)* Why, master Crumbs, be there a spider in the glass?—thee dost not drink. Come, "mercy," man. There be few on us, I fear, would be worse for a little more on't. Tak' another sup.

CRUMBS. No more. There, master Beanstalk, is your receipt—there, friend Thomas, *(giving various papers to farmers.)* is yours. As for that matter about the tithes, master Hodge, we must talk on't. All our business is now despatched, and I'll drain another glass to our next merry-meeting.—*(All rise, having filled glasses.)*

BEAN. Stay. I'll clap a tail to that toast; so drink "good fortune to master Heywood!"

ALL. Ay, ay!

BEAN. Stop. And his wife, Rachel—Not yet!—and all his darling little babes, God bless 'em! *(all drink.)* Why, master Crumbs, what makes thee look so blank?

It be a bad sign if a man make wry faces when he hears luck wished to another.

CRUMBS. Wry faces! you mistake. But you take a good deal of interest in Martin Heywood.

BEAN. Naturally. I ha' known him ever since he could ha' lain in my hat. My dame, here, stood for his wife, Rachel; and a blessed little blossom she was. If it hadn't been for bad times,—but I won't brag. *(Retires amongst Farmers. Second Farmer comes down to Crumbs.)*

2nd FARMER. Now, good master steward, you'll give me time I hope?

CRUMBS. Time is n't in my gift if I would.

2nd FARMER. I have a wife and eight children!

CRUMBS. A marvellous pity; but I must make up my book.

2nd FARMER. Give me but two months.

CRUMBS. You shall have two weeks. Don't reckon on an hour more. Two weeks, and then I sell every stick.

2nd FARMER. Have you no heart?

CRUMBS. I must make up my book!—Two weeks.— *(Farmer retires. Beanstalk, who, with others, has filled his glass, comes down, and forces a glass on Crumbs.)*

BEAN. I say, master Crumbs, the old toast at parting. " Here's mercy to all landlords!"

CRUMBS. *(unwillingly drinking.)* " Mercy—landlords!"—Farewell, farewell!—

All exeunt but CRUMBS.

They're gone; now to sort the money. *(Employs himself sorting papers, notes, &c.)* Heywood must pack. The farm must come into my hands. Let me reckon.

Another twelvemonth,—the landlord still away, and my fortune is complete. I have scraped, and scratched, and wrung!—'Tis very well. Such another year, and farewell England.

Here SILVER JACK and HYSSOP are seen looking in.

JACK. *(pointing out Crumbs to Hyssop.)* 'Tis he! I'll swear it!

CRUMBS. Who's there? *(Jack and Hyssop disappear.)*

Enter STEPHEN, with letters.

Is it you, Stephen?—talking to yourself?

STE. Talking, sir? not I. Here be letters: this, from London; it has our master's crest. *(retires.)*

CRUMBS. Master! Humph! *(opens and reads.)* 'Tis from young Spendthrift. The old style: more money. He shall have it.

TOBY HEYWOOD, without.

TOBY. No, no; I'll walk in. When he sees me, he'll be sure I'm here.

Enters from back.

Servant, master Crumbs.

CRUMBS. Servant; I'd hoped to see your brother, Martin. *(to Stephen, half-aside.)* Stephen, go to Bullfrog. Tell him to come to me to-night; I shall have business for him. Ay, and call on Burly, too, and tell him the same.

Exit STEPHEN.

TOBY. Bullfrog and Burly! What devil's feast's afoot, that they must have a spoon in?

CRUMBS. All trades must be filled: Bullfrog's is an ugly one.

TOBY. Ay; but the ugliest trades have their moments of pleasure. Now, if I were a grave-digger, or even a hangman, there are some people *(glancing at Crumbs.)* I could work for with a great deal of enjoyment.

CRUMBS. That's Bullfrog's maxim: he's very merry.

TOBY. The most jovial of brokers and appraisers. He levies a distress as though he brought a card of invitation; giggles himself into possession; makes out the inventory with a chuckle; and carts off chairs and tables to "Begone dull care!" or, "How merrily we live who Shepherds be."

CRUMBS. True, in these matters he has a coolness.

TOBY. Coolness! he'd eat oysters whilst his neighbour's house was in flames,—always provided that his own was ensured. Coolness! he's a piece of marble, carved into a broad grin!

CRUMBS. Well, well, your business with me?

TOBY. My brother, Martin, has been once more disappointed.

CRUMBS. So have I.

TOBY. That's lucky. You'll be better able to feel for him.

CRUMBS. I want money.

6

TOBY. So does he.

CRUMBS. I'll give time, if there be any one to answer for him. Can't you assist him? have you nothing?

TOBY. Yes: fifteen pounds a-year, as principal usher to the town free-school. My goods and chattels are a volume of " Robinson Crusoe;" ditto " Pilgrim's Progress;" with " Plutarch's Morals," much like the morals of many other people,—a good deal dog's-eared! If my uncle had made me a ploughman instead of a mongrel scholar, I might have had a mouldy guinea or so.

CRUMBS. But has your brother no one to speak for him?

TOBY. Yes. There are two.

CRUMBS. Where shall I find them?

TOBY. In the church-yard. His grandfather and his father lie there. Go to the graves of the old men, and these are the words the dead will say to you: " We lived sixty years in Holly farm. In all that time we never begged an hour of the 'Squire. We paid rent, tax, and tithe: we earned our bread with our own hands, and owed no man a penny when laid down here. Well, then, will ye be hard on young Heywood; will ye press upon our child, our poor Martin, when murrain has come upon his cattle, and blight fallen upon his corn?" This is what the dead will say. I should like to know what the living has to answer?

CRUMBS. *(handing over the Squire's letter.)* This.

TOBY. *(opening it.)* From the young 'Squire. *(reads.)* *" Master Crumbs, use all despatch, and send me, on receipt of this, £500. Cards have tricked me, and the devil logged the dice. Get the money at all costs, and quickly. Robert Grantley."* Ay, a right true letter from an absent landlord.

CRUMBS. 'Tis hard to be steward to a wild youth who looks not after his own estate. You see, he leaves me no discretion?

TOBY. Oh, no. If the landlord lose at gaming, his tenants must suffer for't. The 'Squire plays a low card, —issue a distress-warrant! He throws deuce-ace,— turn a family into the fields! 'Tis only awkward to lose hundreds on a card; but very rascally to be behind-hand with one's rent!

CRUMBS. As you say—very true.—Good morning, master Toby. *(Going.)*

TOBY. Good morning. Poor brother Martin wouldn't come himself, so I thought I'd step up and speak to you. But I'll tell him that you'll give him all time, and that he's not to make himself uneasy, and all that. I'll comfort him, depend on't. And, I say; when you write back to the 'Squire, you can tell him, by way of postscript, if he must feed the gaming-table, not to let it be with money wrung, like blood, from the wretched. Just tell him, whilst he shuffles the cards, to remember the aching hearts of his distressed tenants. And when he'd rattle the dice, let him stop and think of the knuckles of the bailiff and the tax-gatherer, knocking at the cottage-doors of the poor. Good morning, Mr. Steward, good morning.

Exit at back.

CRUMBS. Now to give my instructions to the beadle and appraiser, and out he goes.

Exit.

SCENE II.

A Rustic View.

Enter JACK and HYSSOP.

HYSSOP, *(to Jack, who is looking back).* Come, come, why do you loiter?

JACK. Don't you see that woman still at the stile?—the prettiest creature I've looked on this many a day.

HYS. Tush! now we're on business. Go on with your story. Let me see, where did that wench's black eyes interrupt us? Oh! you were about to tell me how you knew that this steward, Crumbs, as he is called, was your master, when you took to live by your wits and the nimbleness of your five fingers. Now, are you sure you know him?

JACK. Do I know my own hand? Thirty years ago, when but a boy, I ran away from my apprenticeship—

HYS. Ay, of rope-making: a fatal profession. Go on.

JACK. Pshaw! I fell in with John Harris—for that's his real name—in London. He was a knight of the road of the first order; kept as pretty a blood, and shuffled a card better than any baronet of St. James's. Bless you! he gave the fashion to Hounslow and Finchley. Well, Newgate hath clipped many a brave fellow's wing! Captain Harris was taken, tried, and condemned for Tyburn.

HYS. Then he got a reprieve?

JACK. Yes, in the way of some files, sent to him in a pigeon-pie, and twenty fathom of cord, baked in a few loaves. He gave them the slip and started for the Indies. There, I heard, he met with an Englishman, was brought back again, and here he is. Have you a mind to earn fifty pounds?

HYS. If't may be done with the leisure of a gentleman.

JACK. 'Tis but to open your mouth. See: (*takes out a seal-skin tobacco pouch, and from it an old hand bill. Gives it to Hyssop.*) I have worn it about me for many a long day.

HYS. (*Reading bill.*) "*Fifty pounds reward! Escaped from Newgate! John Harris, a convict. He is five feet ten, of a darkish complexion; oval face, quick black eyes, with an eager look: his mouth large and restless; his hair a deep chesnut brown, in close curls. His voice is full and his manner of speaking rapid. His pace short and hurried. Has a scar over the left eye; also a scar on the back of the left hand.*" This can never be the picture of that old man?

JACK. Why, 'tis seven-and-twenty years since he sat for it: that's some time for one who hasn't walked upon velvet. Why, even *I* am changed. I can remember when my mother used to call me her "lovely little Jack." As for Harris, 'twould have done you good to hear him cry " Stand!"—it came sharp upon you like the click of a trigger. Step aside, Hyssop, here are two of the natives. (*they retire amongst the trees.*)

Enter POLLY BRIGGS, BULLFROG following her.

POLLY. Now, Mr. Bullfrog, don't teaze me.

BULL. I teaze! I should like to know how a man with a freehold of twenty pounds per year, a pretty business, and a genteel figure, could teaze, even if he would? It's only poor people who teaze; we monied men delight!

POLLY. Well, I'm very poor, Mr. Bullfrog.

BULL. You are: it's your only fault.

POLLY. Fault! poverty's no crime.

BULL. Isn't it? well, it's so like I don't know the difference. It's a pity poor girls have pretty faces; they lead us prudent capitalists into many false reckonings. Oh, Polly! if I should love you!

POLLY. La! what should you see to love in me?

BULL. See! why, there's a beautiful face with its streaks of red, and the blue veins running up and down the white skin, for all the world like the ruled pages of a new ledger!

POLLY. White skin! Wouldn't you be better pleased if it were yellow?

BULL. La! why?

POLLY. 'Twould remind you of your guineas, you know. And, I'm sure, you love nothing so well.

BULL. Yes, one thing—almost: that pretty little red mouth! Oh, Polly! if you had but a small annuity, or expectations from a sick aunt, or any thing of that kind, you'd be a perfect woman.—But I must have a kiss.

POLLY. A kiss! I never heard of such a thing!

BULL. What an ignorant young woman you must be.

A kiss is——(*Bull is approaching Polly when Toby comes down between them.*)

TOBY. She knows. I taught her long ago. And harkye, Master Bullfrog!

BULL. Now be cool. I'm always cool.

TOBY. You'll still be meddling. Don't you remember that you were *once* kicked?

BULL. Yes. And wasn't I a picture of patience? Did I fly into a rage? No: I flung myself upon the laws. I made twenty pounds by that job, and that didn't make me conceited either.

TOBY. Take care, or I may kick too!

BULL. No. Prudence won't let you.

TOBY. Why not?

BULL. You can't afford to pay for luxuries!

TOBY. Oh! on such an occasion, I'd not mind running in debt! (*to Polly.*) But, Polly, go to the farm; run and comfort Rachel. Leave the appraiser to me. Go.

Exit POLLY.

What! waste your valuable time with a girl not worth a groat?

BULL. That's true. And I ought to be down at Brown's, the millwright's.

TOBY. Ha! no use going there. I'm told they barricade doors and windows. You'll never get in there.

BULL. Ha! ha! You don't know my wit. I took possession this morning.

TOBY. Why, how?

BULL. Such a scheme! About an hour after Brown had let himself out of the window, I got a little girl to go and knock at the door, and call for Mrs. Brown. I taught her her lesson; this was it: "Mrs. Brown, for Heaven's sake!"—I made her say "Heaven," because it sounded more real.

TOBY. Yes, Heaven is a good word to lie under.

BULL. Bless you! I've found it so. "For Heaven's sake come to your husband! he's chopped his leg clean through with an axe!" You should have heard Mrs. Brown scream! Out she ran, wringing her hands,—her three children tumbling after her; and in I and the beadle walked.

TOBY. Then 'twas all a lie?

BULL. Lord love you, only my wit. And so I told Mrs. Brown; and bade her wipe her eyes, and make herself comfortable whilst I took down the goods. I shall sell on Thursday.

TOBY. Sell! You are throwing away your time knocking down tea-cups and wooden dishes. You should go to the colonies and sell the blacks.

BULL. I certainly do pass off an article with a flourish.

TOBY. Flourish! how capitally you'd dispose of a man, his wife, and six children!

BULL. I'm not conceited; but I think I should. Hem! "Ladies and gentlemen, the next lot consists of eight mortals."—Stop, (to Toby.) are blacks mortals?

TOBY. Why, with some, it's a matter of doubt, so let them have the benefit of it.

BULL. "Eight mortals. How much shall we say for the lot?"

TOBY. Or you might ask,—"How much for the man? a strong-bodied labourer, a virtuous husband, and an affectionate father. He weighs fourteen stone, hasn't a single vice, stands five feet eleven, is very handsome, and is going at only a handful of dollars?"

BULL. Must you talk about affection and all that?

TOBY. Of course. Virtue is especially marketable in the West Indies. There, it's worth while being a constant husband and a doating parent; for one sells for a few dollars extra. Go to Jamaica by all means.

BULL. I think I should succeed.

TOBY. Succeed! After your story to Mrs. Brown, if your own father were going by auction, you'd knock him down with the greatest grace in life.

BULL. Now, you flatter!

TOBY. Impossible. With you, there's no improving upon truth.

BULL. Well, that's really handsome. But I——

Enter CRUMBS.

Good day, master Crumbs. I was coming, by your order, about——

CRUMBS. In good time. (*seeing Toby.*) He here!

TOBY. Don't let me interrupt business. I'm going to the farm. Good bye, Bullfrog; and, I say, if, in the course of auction matters you've a lot of humanity to dispose of——

BULL. Well?

TOBY. Think of Mrs. Brown, and buy it in for yourself!

Exit.

CRUMBS. A subtle, sneering rogue, that. Harkye, Bullfrog, you must this day seize on Heywood's goods. (*Silver Jack and Hyssop come down.*) Strangers here!

JACK. (*slapping Crumbs on the back.*) Your servant, old sir!

CRUMBS. Old sir!

JACK. Ay. There's no shame in grey hairs, is there? even though they once were a chesnut-brown. (*sarcastically.*) What then? hair will change.

HYS. Yes, and quick black eyes, with an eager look, will grow dim and dull.

JACK. A deep voice will lose something of its music; and five feet ten shrink into (*measuring Crumbs with his eye.*) five feet seven or eight.

HYS. A large and restless mouth *may* last.

JACK. Ay, and scars, (*seizing the hand of Crumbs, who stands amazed and trembling.*) Yes, scars will not rub out!

CRUMBS. Villains! robbers! (*passionately.*)

BULL. Robbers! shall I call the constable?

CRUMBS. Peace! away! (*is hurrying off: Jack arrests him.*)

JACK. Nay, nay, old gentleman; we are strangers, and ask a day's hospitality at the mansion.

CRUMBS. (*still terrified, and endeavouring to escape.*) Away—away!

JACK. (*holding him.*) As you will not give us house-room, will you tell me where I may find a printer?—I wish to distribute through the village some hundred copies of this little bill. (*shows Crumbs the hand-bill: he staggers back confounded.*)

BULL. A printer! My cousin Hairspace is the man. Does all my catalogues. Give me the bill. (*is about to take the bill.*)

CRUMBS. Touch it not; touch it not, I say! Come, gentlemen! (*inviting them on.*)

JACK. Nay, we will not trouble you. (*to Bull.*) Your cousin, you say?——

BULL. The best printer forty miles about. In black, blue, or red ink, plain or ornamental,—there is no printer who—(*endeavouring to get the bill.*)

CRUMBS. The devil seize thee,—peace!—Come, gentlemen; nay, you must with me to the mansion. We will have a brave dinner! Some wine! wine! I do entreat you not to stay, my good friends.—(*Anxiously endeavouring to lead Jack and Hyssop off.*)

JACK. As you're so pressing;—but we shall trouble you.

CRUMBS. No, no; it gladdens me that I have met you. Come.

BULL, (*who creeps round to Jack and gives him a card.*) My cousin's card.

CRUMBS. (*Crossing to Bullfrog.*) What dost mutter?

BULL. Mutter! La! Mr. Crumbs! I only presented Timothy's card. Must always think of trade, you know.

CRUMBS. (*With extreme passion.*) Think of trade! wouldst see me hanged?

BULL. No. I never neglect business for pleasure.

CRUMBS. Beware! beware! and follow me! (*To Jack and Hyssop,*) Come, gentlemen; come, my good friends! Nay, you first; I entreat.

Exit CRUMBS, bowing off JACK and HYSSOP, who exchange looks.

BULL. Beware—beware—to a freeholder! I'll——no—I'm not yet rich enough to be in a passion. When I've made my fortune, then I may indulge in the feelings of a gentleman.

Exit.

SCENE III.

A Rustic Landscape.—Evening.

RACHEL discovered, seated on the projecting step of a stile at the side.

RACH. The sun is almost set, and yet I see not Martin. Oh! my dear husband! my poor children! heaven be kind to us,—for I've almost lost all other hope.—Ha! Martin! Martin!

MARTIN HAYWOOD appears at the stile :—crosses it.

MARTIN. Rachel here! — Why did you leave the farm?

RACH. I could not stay there and you away. Our children, Martin; they cried for you. I could not speak to them; I could not stay. Now, Martin, your friend?

MAR. (*with bitterness.*) Friend!

RACH. Oh! do not look so—do not.

MAR. I have done that to-day I never did before; I have wished myself dead! ay, dead! that I might be quit of all.

RACH. And our children, Martin?

MAR. 'Twould be better for 'em. There's some spell upon me! Do what I will it does not thrive! Why, 'tis certain there's some curse upon me!

RACH. Be patient, dear Martin!

MAR. Patient! I have been patient. Harvest after harvest's failed;—flock after flock has died; yet have I smiled upon't, and gone whistling 'bout the fields. I have been hunted by landlord—threatened by the taxman— yet I've put a stout heart upon't, and never drooped. Rachel Heywood, you see me now without a shilling— without a home—my children with not a week's food before them—my wife starving—and yet I'm patient.

RACH. I never saw you so till now. Martin, what has happened?

MAR. I may sit down and see my little ones pine day by day; I may feel their wasting limbs, and hear them scream for bread; and I may stare in their white faces, and tell them to be patient. Patient!

RACH. Look not so fiercely at me, Martin. Are they not my children—mine? Am I not their mother? Can your love be more than mine? But no; you did not mean that. Come, Martin, be not so hasty. What has happened?

MAR. No matter; let it rest with me.

RACH. But it must not, Martin. How many a time have you said that you could have no secret from Rachel?

MAR. I don't remember that.

RACH. Look there, Martin, (*pointing to the stile.*)— How often have we met at yonder stile ; how often have we waited there for hours, and talked of our wedding-day and all our hopes?—then you have said————

MAR. Ay, those were gay days! Then, life seemed

D

full of promise, as a field of ripened corn. Those were happy times!

RACH. They will come back, never fear it. Now tell me, Martin, have you been to your friend?

MAR. I have been to Harry Wilson. The same Harry Wilson to whom my grandfather lent good guineas to begin the world.

RACH. You asked him to lend you the money for a time?

MAR. I stammered it out somehow.

RACH. And did he?

MAR. Damn him!

RACH. Oh, Martin!

MAR. I thought I was talking to a brother. I told him all, Rachel, all!—And he heard me, with a smile on his face, and said, he was sorry!

RACH. Then he could not assist us?

MAR. No. His money was laid out in ventures,—he had lost by lending;—but he was very sorry!

RACH. And he offered nothing?

MAR. When I told him we had not a guinea,—not a home that we could call ours,—not a certain meal,—the tears came into my eyes, and I felt like a thief whilst I said all this;—well, he wouldn't lend me a farthing: but, kind soul! he bade me take a glass of wine, and hope for better days! I took the wine, and pouring it upon the floor, wished that my blood might be so poured out from my heart if ever again I stood beneath his roof; and so I left him!

RACH. And your other friend?

MAR. No: I asked no other. One denial was enough.

RACH. Then every hope is gone!

MAR. No; there is one hope yet. And yet I cannot

bear to think of it. Rachel, our children must not starve.
—What say you, shall we cross the sea?

RACH. What! leave the farm?

MAR. I am offered a place on an estate, far away in
the Indies. What say you?

RACH. Leave this place?

MAR. Why not? We shall find sun and sky and
green fields there.

RACH. But not our own fields, not our own sky,—
not the friends who love us, not the neighbours who
respect us. Oh! think not of it. Our children! they
would die there! Die amongst strangers! Martin, would
you quit our home?

MAR. Our home! where is it?—the work-house!—
Ha! ha!—Our home! Rachel, it shall be. We'll not
be pointed at as beggars. We'll be no burden to the
parish. We'll take our children in our arms, and leave
this place for ever——

Enter TOBY HEYWOOD.

TOBY. Leave this place! what for, Martin; have you
got scent of a gold-mine?

RACH. Oh, speak to him—persuade him! He would
go from here—go, and die in some foreign place!

TOBY. Nay, he has more wisdom than that. Thou'rt
not such a fool, Martin. Come, I'll give you better
advice.

MAR. Spare it for those who ask it: I want none.

TOBY. Come, don't snub your younger brother. If
you did enter the world ten months and a few seconds
before me, you can hear reason. Go to foreign parts,
eh?

MAR. Shall I stay here and starve?

TOBY. Come, Martin, we never looked sulkily at one another when we were boys; now, 'twould be too late to begin: we should make no hand of it. Starve!

MAR. Ay. Will not the steward seize?

TOBY. No, no. I have been and talked to him.

MAR. You didn't beg for?——

TOBY. Beg! There's little of the beggar in my face: I talked reason to him. I said, a man who hadn't money, couldn't well pay any. All you wanted was time; and he didn't refuse.

RACH. There, Martin; I told you not to be cast down. I knew we should yet be happy.

MAR. Still there is no certainty that——

TOBY. I tell you what, brother; you are one of those people who are so very fond of ill-luck, that they run half-way to meet it. Old Crumbs will give you time—I know it. Go, Rachel; go to the farm. Wipe your eyes, kiss the babies, take down the bacon; draw a mug of nut-brown, and Martin and I will find appetites. There, away with you.

RACH. You will follow, Martin? There, look light again. That's well. We shall once more be happy— very happy! Fortune will change, be sure of it.

Exit.

TOBY. Change! to be sure she will. Fortune's a wo- man! Hang it, Martin, do muster up a laugh. There, now,—practise that fifty times a-day, and care would as soon be hanged as dare to look at you! (*Toby, clapping Martin on the shoulder, gradually rouses him into cheer- fulness, and Exeunt.*)

SCENE IV.

The old Oak Room in Grantley's Mansion. The Pannels elaborately carved, in the antique style. In one of the compartments, a Picture of a young Female, richly habited.

Enter GRANTLEY, shewn in by BULLFROG, who is slightly intoxicated.

BULL. Master Crumbs will be with you, sir, in the knocking-down of a hammer. From London, sir?

GRAN. I am. A fine old mansion this.

BULL. Beautiful! Capital piece of oak-tree pannelling that: nice bold carving, sir. (*pointing to figures.*) Pretty cherubim's heads in the corners. That's a figure of Mercy. Should like to have the selling of the house and furniture.

GRAN. The owner is indebted to your good wishes.

BULL. The owner! Oh! he's a wild fellow. He's never among us. No, sir; he's a London spark. His father left him abroad: and, though the old man's been dead, and the young gentleman's been in England these two years, he has never paid us a visit.

GRAN. Fond of a town life, I suppose?

BULL. Very fond. And then he's so lucky in his steward.

GRAN. Indeed!

BULL. Oh! he's a jewel of a man!—so punctual with the tenants. There's no keeping a guinea from him, sir He's a delightful man for our business.

GRAN. And your profession is——

BULL. (*giving card.*) Appraiser and auctioneer. Happy to serve you. I made one seizure this morning, shall make another to-night. If you've thoughts of staying amongst us, and want to furnish, I can assist you to two or three good penn'orths. (*Grantley has been observing the picture.*) What, sir! you are looking at that picture? I don't know the painter. It's not a——

GRAN. No——(*musing.*)

BULL. No. And it's not by—by—(*aside.*)—I must get an Italian smatter, or I shall never be able to knock down the painters!

GRAN. Is it a family portrait?

BULL. Why, sir, between ourselves, if I were to put it up for auction, I should call it a conundrum in an oak frame!

GRAN. Why so?

BULL. Why, more than twice, I've caught Mr. Crumbs standing before it looking at it;—and once (you'll hardly believe it, for nobody who knows him would), I caught him with the tears rolling down his cheeks. Nobody would believe it!

GRAN. Then he's not generally given to strong emotion?

BULL. Bless you! no, sir. He's too much a man of business for that. Here he comes. Not a word.

Enter CRUMBS from Centre Door in Scene.

CRUMBS. Your servant, sir. Business must excuse me that I made you wait. (*to Bull.*) Go you and see that Burly is at hand. I seize within this hour. Go!

BULL. I will;—(*aside.*)—but first for the other bottle with Captain Jack. I must better my taste in wines, if only in the way of trade.

Exit at door.

GRAN. I shall tax your hospitality for some days. This (*giving a letter.*) from my friend, Grantley.

CRUMBS. He's well, I trust? (*aside.*) Curses on it. (*reads.*) "*The bearer is my most special friend: treat him with all respect as he were myself. He will stay to sport some week or two.*" I would, sir, we had had earlier notice. I fear me you will find us ill-provided.

GRAN. Never fear it.

CRUMBS. In truth, sir, 'tis a dull spot. Here we see no one—hear no one.

GRAN. Indeed it seems still enough.

CRUMBS. You never hear a sound—not a sound; unless it be the birds in the rookery, or, at night, a mouse scratching in the wall. (*loud laughing and knocking within. Silver Jack sings, in a loud voice:*

"May corn never fail; for that makes good ale,
But a blight to all hempseed, brave boys, brave boys;
But a blight to all hempseed, brave boys!——

(*laughing and noise.*)

GRAN. Do the mice scratch thus early?

CRUMBS, (*confused.*) I—I—(*Laughing and noise continued.*)

GRAN. The rooks are somewhat jovial.

CRUMBS. It hath never happened until now. They are the richest of the 'Squire's tenants—devout religious men;—but to-day being rent day——

JACK and HYSSOP are heard at the door.

Holloa, Master Crumbs.

CRUMBS. I come—I—(*to Grant.*) Men of worth and reputation.

JACK. (*At door.*) Master Crumbs! John Harris! Fifty pounds reward!

CRUMBS. Damnation! (*In extreme terror rushes up and opens folding doors in scene. Silver Jack and Hyssop are seen, with Bullfrog trying to keep them back. They come down, all flushed with wine, Jack holding a bottle.*)

CRUMBS. (*Aside to them.*) I am busy. I will return. Go.

JACK. Busy! Damn business!

BULL. No: don't damn business. I'm very drunk, but I can't damn business: it's profane.

JACK. To leave your company, and—(*seeing Grantley.*) Oh! a gentleman! Introduce us. You won't? no?— I'll introduce myself—(*puts bottle upon the stage, which Bullfrog takes up, and retires to back; seats himself in chair, and, during the following, drinks till he falls asleep.*) Servant, sir. Nice house this. Capital wine; yes, and a civil steward.—Sir, I beg your friendship. If you're for any thing in this way, I——(*taking from his pocket a pack of cards, and shuffling them.*)

HYS. Ay, sir; or if there be music in this—(*rattling a dice box.*)

GRAN. (*aside.*) Devout, religious men!

JACK. We're not avaricious. We play for anything, from a marvedi to a thousand guineas.

CRUMBS. (*who has been vainly endeavouring to keep them back.*) No, no; the gentleman does not play. Go in, my good friends.

GRAN. (*to Crumbs.*) With your leave, I'll look about the grounds.

JACK. Fine spot, nice house, good wine,—ay, and (*looking at portrait,*) pretty pictures! Well, I say, (*to Hyssop.*) isn't that an angel?

HYS. I can't say: I've not been used to such company.

GRAN. It is, indeed, beautiful. (*to Crumbs,*) Tell me, whose portrait is it? Did you know the lady?

CRUMBS. (*with suppressed emotion.*) She was a—a favourite of the late 'Squire's. She's long since dead.

JACK. A favourite and dead! Ha! I suppose the 'Squire was fond of her, and so broke her heart.

CRUMBS. (*with passion.*) How dare you——

JACK. (*coolly and in an under tone.*) Come, come, John Harris; fifty pounds reward!

CRUMBS. (*recovering himself, to Grantley.*) Come, sir, I will show you——

GRAN. Do not quit your friends. With your leave, I'll go alone. Gentlemen, I am the humblest of your servants. (*Aside.*) Devout, religious men!

Exit.

HYS. A pretty spoken fellow.

JACK. And a rich one. Did you see the diamonds on his fingers? I warrant me his pockets are—umph! a prize? (*To Crumbs.*) What say you?

E

CRUMBS. I—I?——

JACK. I'd forgot. You only rob now as a steward. You're one of the regulars.

CRUMBS. Rob! harkye!——

JACK. Come, come, John Harris; no big words. I've something here, (*showing the bill,*) wouldn't look so well framed as that red-lipped young lady. (*pointing to picture.*)

CRUMBS. Well, well, we're friends; but be cautious, I implore you. (*In great agitation.*) Come, you shall have more wine, wine!

JACK. Wine! Ay, we will have more. And then for our plans, old boy; then for our plans. Why, how lucky it was that we met one another! You see there were a few pressing inquiries about us in London, so we thought we'd take the benefit of country air, until the anxiety of our friends cooled a little. But then to think of the luck of our meeting! Ar'n't you delighted? (*Embracing him.*)

CRUMBS. Yes, yes. But go in. You shall have wine. I'll go see to it.

JACK. Wine, wine! Ha! ha! We drink courage with wine. Success to the grapes,——(*Sings*)

> "But a blight to all hempseed, brave boys, brave boys,
> A blight to all hempseed, brave boys!"

CRUMBS forces JACK and HYSSOP into room in scene.

CRUMBS. The devil has forsaken me! To be tracked out after so many years! This visitor, too! No; my course is clear. But how to dispose of that ruffian? Ha! he has been prating of some woman;—by the description 'tis Heywood's wife.—I'll put him in possession of the farm, and thus rid me of him, whilst I—let me see——

BULL. (*still asleep.*) What shall we say for this wine, fifty years in bottle? Thank'e, sir; it's going,—going,—gone. (*Lets the bottle fall out of his hand.*)

CRUMBS, (*who has remained in a state of deep thought, startled, rushes up to Bullfrog, and seizes him.*) Scoundrel! Listening!

BULL. Dreaming—only dreaming. I just knocked down the sweetest ten dozen!——

CRUMBS. Up, or I strangle you! Is't thus you mind your business?

BULL. Business!—that's enough. Cry business!—and, if I don't move, you may send for the undertaker.

CRUMBS. Hence!

BULL. I'm going. Business is business. Capital wine. (*sings:*)

"And a blight to all hempseed," &c. &c.

CRUMBS. Hence! hence!——(*forces him off.*)

SCENE V.

The Interior of Heywood's Farm. The Scene, Furniture, &c. as in WILKIE's *Picture of* "DISTRAINING FOR RENT." *Martin and Rachel seated at Table, with Toby, Beanstalk, his Dame, and the Children. Ale, Jugs, &c. on the Table.*

BEAN. Come, Martin, here be better times.—So: we shall be jovial yet, man.

RACH. Ay, that we shall; and so I tell him, farmer; but he will not heed me.

MAR. We have had nought but ill-luck since the old man died.

BEAN. Why, 'twas awfully sudden, to be sure.

MAR. Here he was one minute as strong and as lightsome as ever; when death fell upon him like a bolt, and he lay upon that bed, panting, like a run-down hare.

TOBY. Odd's, Martin! look into your ale: you'll see something better than dying men. Our grandfather's in heaven. Here's to the memory of him! Let him rest.

MAR. I tell you I can't but think of him. Abroad or at home I see him. Sometimes, when I'm falling into sleep, his eyes seem to stare close at my face, and I start and gasp again; and then I see him looking and pointing at that chair. (*to farmer*.) You know, farmer, he'd sit in it for hours, with one of the youngsters on his knee.— Still I see him with his hand stretched forth, and his throat working, as though the words were there but couldn't out;—and so he died. Depend on't, there was something on the old man's mind.

TOBY. Brother, shall I go to the church-yard and bring you a skull and cross-bones? for, in your present humour, they're your fittest company.

MAR. I'm a fool to think so. (*fills horn*.) Come, farmer, your hand; Toby, yours; Rachel, lass, we'll be merry yet. Here's to better times! (*drinks, then takes two of the children upon his knees*.)

TOBY. Come, I warrant me, there's more comfort in that than in ghosts' eyes at midnight. Why, it's up in your cheek already, man. Take another.

MAR. With all my heart. And again I'll drink, "here's better times!"

Enter POLLY BRIGGS at Door.

POLLY. Oh, farmer Heywood! Here comes the steward and that nasty appraiser, and the beadle; and all the folks say they're coming here to seize!——

MAR. (*putting down the children*.) Rachel, stand aside!—that gun!—(*is going to take the gun from over the chimney-piece; Rachel prevents him*.)

RACH. Oh, Martin! husband! for the love of heaven!—

TOBY. What would you, Martin?

MAR. Shoot the first man who crosses yonder threshold. Let me go!

BEAN. Come, come, Martin, be not rash: thee'st no reason to be so.

MAR. No reason! You have a wife and children, yet say I have no reason!—Are not here five—(*pointing. to Rachel and children.*)—five bitter reasons? The gun! (*violently.*)

TOBY. Martin, Martin, are you mad?

MAR. (*falling despairingly into a chair.*) I am mad. God help me!—I am mad!

Enter CRUMBS at Door.

CRUMBS. This is a disagreeable business.

TOBY. I should know that by your looking so pleased.

CRUMBS. I want my due.

TOBY. You'll have it some day. I wish the law. allowed me to give it you now.

BEAN. Come, come, master Crumbs; have compassion.

TOBY. Compassion!—Tell him to have three heads.

RACH. Do not anger him. (*to Crumbs.*) Good sir, give us time: but a short time: have mercy.—Kneel, children, kneel! (*Children are about to kneel, when Martin starts forward.*)

MAR. Stand! if you're of my blood. They are the children of an honest man, and must not kneel before a villain!

CRUMBS. Mighty well. You owe a twelvemonth's. rent; and, instead of money, you give blustering words. Rent-day passes lightly with you.

MAR. Lightly! (*to Bean.*) Farmer, as I am a man, I have lived a whole year in torment. Day has been all misery to me, and bed no bed. Still, as rent-day would come, I have lain awake whole nights, and every night was more dreadful than the past. Then I've tried to, think no more, but dug my head into my pillow and fixed my fingers tightly in my hair, and tried to stun myself to sleep;—but all would not do.—There appeared a something hanging over me—about me;—heavy and stifling it seemed,—and my blood would run hot and cold; and so I've lain and watched, and prayed the daylight in. The next night worse, for it brought the time still nearer. And when at last the rent-day came, and I without one groat, I've crossed yon door, not with an English farmer's tread, but with a thief's pace, crawling to the gallows!—This is to pass rent-day lightly!

CRUMBS. Why not give up the farm? Why not leave the house?

MAR. Why not? My father's father grew grey under this roof. And sooner should these beams fall and knock my brains out than I would quit them. Here I was born, and here I will die. If you would take me through yon door, master Crumbs, I tell you it must be heels foremost. Leave the house! I almost love it like a living thing.

CRUMBS. All very fine. For my part, I can't see why one house shouldn't be as good as another.

MAR. Likely you cannot. But I have crawled a little child upon this floor: the very door-step is worn with my feet. I have seen my mother, fathers, die here!—I—I tell you here I first saw the light, and here I'll close my eyes.

RACH. Dear Martin, be calm.

CRUMBS. You'll not oppose the law?

MAR. I know not that. I tell you, don't provoke me. (*taking the arm-chair.*) Here I sit—in my grandfather's chair: the chair of that old man, who, for forty years, paid rent and tithe to the last guinea. Here I sit! And I warn you, put not a hand upon a stick or thread!

CRUMBS. (*calling at door.*) Come in, friends.

Enter BULLFROG and BURLY at Door.

MAR. I warn you back.

BURLY. (*shewing a paper.*) What say you to our warrant, master Heywood?

MAR. I tell you not to tempt me. I cannot trust myself, for I am desperate! Leave the farm!

CRUMBS. (*to Bull and Burly.*) You know your duties.

Exit through Door.

BULL. (*who has been looking over goods.*) Business is business. (*takes out pen, ink, and book.*) One bedstead!

MAR. Let me come at them!

TOBY. Nay, nay, brother!

RACH. Husband!

CHILDREN. Father! (*they all hang about Martin, keeping him from attacking Burly and Bullfrog.*

MAR. (*after a struggle, sinks into the chair.*) Rachel! —my poor babes!—take all, take all!

BULL. (*making out the inventory.*) One bedstead!— one table!

BEANSTALK and NEIGHBOURS, who have entered.

Shame! shame!

TOBY. Blood-suckers!

BULL. One toasting-fork, one bird-cage, one baby's rattle!

MAR. God help us! God help us! (*buries his face in his hands. Bullfrog seats himself on bed; and other Characters so arrange themselves as to represent* WILKIE'S *Picture of "* DISTRAINING FOR RENT*".*)

END OF ACT I.

ACT THE SECOND.

Scene First.   The Interior of Heywood's Farm.   Day breaking.   The Furniture of the Scene as at the conclusion of the First Act.   Polly Briggs discovered, seated at a Table.   A light burning.

POLLY.   Dear me! how heavily the time goes,—and the farm,—I declare it doesn't look as it used to do.   I'm so tired—yet I must keep my eyes open for company's sake.

Enter RACHEL.

RACH.   They sleep soundly.   Poor children!   Heaven knows where they will rest another night.   I stood and watched them; and they looked so innocent—so happy.—they smiled, and my heart died within me.

POLLY.   Don't take on so.   Martin will return with good news, never fear.

RACH.   I'm so wretched, I have lost even hope.—My pretty babes, had we been always beggars, then you could have borne cold, nipping winds, rough words, uncertain

F

food;—but now, they'll pine, and so they'll die. Even our children will be taken from us.

POLLY. Well, I never thought you could talk after this fashion.

RACH. Nor I. But then I had not seen my infants lying on a bed no longer theirs.—Is it not almost day-break? Had Martin been successful, he would surely have been back.

POLLY. Now why will you think the worst? I shouldn't wonder if he returned with a large bag of money. I'll go to the end of the lane, and see if either he or Toby be coming.

RACH. No, do not leave me—the stranger up stairs —Yet go; but do not stay.

Exit POLLY *at door.*

Sure the morning will never come. Oh, yes, 'twill come too soon. Then another and another, and we are house-less beggars. I walk about the place like a restless ghost.—To know the worst were better than to remain thus. (*Sits down.*) I am worn and tired—even too tired to sleep. (*Fatigued, she falls asleep.*)

Enter SILVER JACK, *cautiously.*

JACK. All quiet. Harris must have put some devil into that wine, or I had never slept so. Here am I in possession,—a watch-dog over spoons and platters, whilst Hyssop, I warrant me, is rarely plucking that new-comer. Jack, Jack, so it has ever run; a pair of bright eyes has been a will-o'-the-wisp to you, leading you through quag-mires all your life.—Ha! (*seeing Rachel.*) she's here and sleeping! How tired, pale, yet pretty she seems! She looks good, and—pshaw! we all look good asleep. How still the place is; no one here but ourselves:—yes, the children. I just passed through their room, and saw them looking as fresh and as rosy—I felt as I hadn't felt for many a day.—'Twas a fool's moment, and is gone.— (*Approaching her; she wakes.*)

Rach. Martin, Martin! (*Seeing Jack.*) You here!

Jack. I couldn't well sleep, so I thought I'd come down and keep you company. This is a much pleasanter room.

Rach. It is at your service. I can go to my children's. (*Going.*)

Jack. (*staying her.*) They're all fast asleep. Bless their little hearts! I stood and looked at them just now till I quite loved them. They are very handsome.

Rach. And most unfortunate.

Jack. Why this is an awkward business. But you may yet find friends.

Rach. Friendship!

Jack. We sometimes find it where we had least thoughts of it. Your children are very like you.

Rach. It has been remarked. I—(*going.*)

Jack. (*lingering.*) Yes, full purses ought to go with full hearts.

Rach. 'Twould save much misery. I would your employer——

Jack. My employer! Why, to be sure, old Crumbs was once my master: but times are changed; we are now bosom friends. I am only here to oblige him.

Rach. Your task can hardly be a pleasant one.

Jack. Nay, 'tis very pleasant. Look you, I have been rolling these many years about the world, and this *(displaying a purse)* has still been gathering. Those pretty babes of yours,—I'm mightily taken with them.—Where is your husband?

RACH. Gone, as a last hope, to try to borrow. He should have been back by this.

JACK. I never found this purse so troublesome before. Will you lighten it for me? Come, no ceremony. You want money: I don't.

RACH. Oh! this is kind, most kind. Yet from a stranger——

JACK. Pshaw! Ill-fortune, now and then, makes sudden acquaintances. *(Still pressing the money.)*

RACH. Indeed, sir, I—I cannot.

JACK. Yet the poor babes must sleep somewhere tomorrow. Come!

RACH. My husband will speedily be here; he, perhaps——

JACK. Nay, when I'm in the humour, I wouldn't be balked. Now, or never. Hang it! take the purse.— *(Forces the purse into her hand.)*

RACH. My husband will return it with a thousand thanks. My children are saved. Oh! you have made us most happy!

JACK. That's enough for me. As for returning the money, that may rest with yourself. 'Twould have been hard for you to see your husband in a jail; yourself and little ones without a home.

RACH. Only to hear you name it, makes me tremble.

JACK. But there's no such hard fortune for you. No: you may stay in your farm, have your children about you, whilst all fears of beggary and the workhouse——why, you seem ill?

RACH. The sudden joy—'tis nothing, and will pass.

JACK. Come, sit down—*(she sits.)*—There, you are looking better whilst I speak, *(hanging over the chair.)* As for the money, if you like to have it as a gift, 'tis a bargain between us. So, to make it binding, just one kiss!—*(throwing his arms about her: she shrinks from him.)* Why do you look so at me?

RACH. I was deceived! I thought I saw a friend: I was deceived!—*(rising.)*

JACK. Tush! I am your friend. Come, one kiss.

RACH. There *(dropping the purse at his feet)* is your money. *(going.)*

JACK. Will you be blind to your own good? I tell you the money shall be yours—all yours. I care not for a penny of it.

RACH. Be silent, and let me go. *(endeavouring to pass.)*

JACK. Think of your children—your husband——*(seizes her.)*

RACH. I do, and scorn you. *(breaking from him.)*

JACK. Are you mad?—listen to my offer.

RACH. Had you made it when the world went well with us—when this roof sheltered a happy family—when every day brought its plenty, its content—when we had no fear of poverty or persecution—even then, the thought of that you purpose should have brought the blushes to your face, and made you dumb with shame;—but now,—with want at our hearth—a husband mad with sorrow—children unprotected—now to offer!—oh! you have a heart of stone, or you could ne'er have thought it.

JACK. Hear reason, and take the purse. I tell you I do not mean——

RACH. You mean the worst. He who would destroy

a happy fire-side, is vile and infamous; but he who insults its wretchedness, is base indeed.

JACK. Base! Look you!—zounds! to be whipped by a woman's tongue! Come, don't let us part so. This is all very well, but, but—hang it! can't we understand one another?

RACH. Oh! Martin! Martin!

JACK. (*chinking the purse.*) He may sleep in a prison to-morrow!

RACH. Let me pass. I must, will go to my children.

JACK. (*throwing up the purse.*) And they may want a breakfast.

RACH. Villain! though you insult the wife, have pity on the mother. (*attempting to cross, he seizes her.*) Let me go!

JACK. Not now—I have gone too far.

RACH. Oh! you will not! Mercy! Martin! (*despairingly.*) He comes not!

JACK. (*passionately.*) You may rave. You've roused me, and I'll not be trifled with.

RACH. Help! help! (*they struggle.*) My husband! —he is here!——(*Jack, surprised, lets her go, and falls back. She rushes to the door, and seizes a woodcutter's bill that is lying on some wood near the wall.*)

JACK. Tricked!

RACH. You see a sound will make a coward of the wicked. Do not come near me; pray do not. This, though you die, shall protect me.

JACK. Well, well, I own I've been wrong—I ask pardon. Come back. Put your trust——

RACH. In this! (*lifting the bill.*) I say again, stir not! Stay beneath this roof! Stay in the poor man's house you would have outraged! Stay,—blush,—and beg to be forgiven!

Exit through Door.

JACK. Gone!—what devil is it that cows me? Ha! *(looking out.)* She flies down the lane. That copse!—yes, though I ran to the gallows, I would follow her.

Exit through Door.

BULL. *(putting his head from between the bed curtains.)* Run to the gallows!—you needn't hurry yourself; the gallows will wait for you. Well, this I call an adventure! Now, if this cause come to trial, I'm witness ready for either side. As I'm a sworn appraiser it's almost daylight!—why, I must have been asleep these seven or eight hours, and nobody knew it. This all comes of the steward's wine. Eh? I hear a footstep. I must sleep and listen. *(disappears.)*

Enter POLLY at Door.

POLLY. Why, Rachel! Oh! gone up stairs, I suppose, to cry over the poor little things! Well, I've no good news for her. I went all down the lane, and came back over the fields, and saw no signs of Martin or Toby either. If these are the troubles that are to come upon the married, I'm sure a poor girl is better single. There's nothing but vexation in this world!—and, dear me, I'm so sleepy!—I haven't had a single wink all night, and it's a shame, too; for there stood the bed so inviting, as though it said, do come and lie down! There'll be no harm in sitting upon it. *(sits on the bed.)* How I should like to lie down!

BULL. *(putting his head through the curtains.)* Well, there's plenty of room for two!

POLLY. *(screaming and running into corner.)* Thieves! Murder!——

At this instant TOBY appears at the Door.

TOBY. Polly!—Bullfrog!

POLLY. Oh! the wretch!

TOBY. *(seizing Bullfrog.)* What's this?—speak!

BULL. How can I, with your fingers in my windpipe?

TOBY. *(dragging him out of bed.)* Answer me: what is all this?

POLLY. Yes, explain, Mr. Bullfrog.

BULL. *(half-aside to Polly.)* Don't be a fool, and nobody will be the wiser.

POLLY. The wiser, sir?—the wiser!

TOBY. Speak, I say!

BULL. *(aside.)* Now I'll talk nettles to him. Well, Mr. Heywood; the fact is I—I am but man.

TOBY. Why, no; I never took you for an angel.

BULL. Perhaps not, Mr. Heywood; but the fair sex—*(winking to Polly)*—the fair sex can discover modest merit.

POLLY. Now, as I'm alive, I was here alone,—and never knowing that that wretch——

BULL. Fie! wretch? What *now!* call me wretch now?

POLLY. That monster!——

BULL. Come, no scandal. If you will tell the truth, I can't help it; but no scandal.

POLLY. That—that——

BULL. There, don't press her: you see her feelings—

TOBY. Master Bullfrog, you've had a marvellous escape.

BULL. How?

TOBY. In not lighting on as great a fool as yourself: else, my life on't, your head had been broken.

BULL. A fool! And have you the audacity to call me a fool?

TOBY. And not all fool: for the rogue is so equally mixed, that there's no saying where either begins or ends.

BULL. Fool! rogue!—The law will tell you this is slander.

TOBY. I know it: I'm speaking the truth.

BULL. And the law shall mend my character.

TOBY. The character that needs law to mend it, is hardly worth the tinkering. In one word, how came you here?

POLLY. That's right. Make him tell you.

BULL. Tell! well, you're a courageous woman! What, then (*to Toby.*) you've no suspicion?—there's no making you unhappy?

TOBY. No.

BULL. Mrs. Heywood will be a fortunate woman.

TOBY. What put you into that bed?

POLLY. Yes, what put you into that bed?

BULL. If you must know,—this. (*producing bottle from his pocket.*) This put me to bed: it's done as much for many a man.

TOBY. What do you mean?

BULL. Mean?—Didn't I attend here as sworn appraiser, and didn't I make the inventory? Yes. (*producing it.*) Here it is: " One cradle, one toasting fork," —all right; move a stick, and I'll indict you! Well,

G

there was a great noise in the family; one running one way—one another,—children crying—women fainting, a smell of burnt feathers; and your brother swearing, enough to shock any christian, who knows what virtue is, and pays his way. I had brought a little wine from the mansion, and, all of a sudden, I found myself quite alone here, so I sat down upon the bed, and I drank and drank. Then I got on the bed, then between the blankets, pulled-to the curtains, looked at my inventory— (some of the things will sell well)—said my prayers,— droned a hymn, and went to sleep! Then,—no I pass over the rest—when you came in, you—but I mustn't go any further.

TOBY. Yes, you must.

BULL I tell you I can't.

TOBY. I tell you you must—you must go over that door-step. If you remain here two minutes longer, 'twill not be on your legs, I promise you. (*menacing him.*)

BULL. I give you warning! Remember, I'm a sworn appraiser.

TOBY. You're the better able to judge for what you ought to be knocked down.—Come, pack!

BULL. I'm going. But only threaten me, and I'll call down the man from up-stairs—he who's in possession.— (*Aside.*) They mustn't know he's gone, or they'll block up the premises.

TOBY. (*still threatening him.*) I've given you fair words.

BULL. Keep to 'em: you can't do better. Ha! drop your arm, or I call for the man. If you put me in bodily fear, it's no fault of mine!—Now, Mr. Toby!—here! my good man—(*Shrinking from Toby, and feigning to call down Silver Jack.*) My good man!

TOBY. Will you go?

BULL. I will, *(aside)* to give Crumbs notice. Ha! I'll call!—I tell you I'll call. As for that young woman, if you demand any satisfaction?—oh! you don't? well, it's very prudent, of you.—Don't stir a step, or down he comes. And now—now *(aside,)* to put another man in. (*Bull. gets to door, stops, and calls as to man up-stairs,*) My good man, see that they don't move a stick! *(Toby runs to door, and Bullfrog makes his escape.)*

POLLY. If you'll believe me, my dear Toby, I never dreamt that that wretch—that villain—that—

TOBY. I'm sure you must be intimate with him by the correctness of your description. Let the fool go. Where's Rachel?

POLLY. With the children. Have you seen nothing of Martin?

TOBY. No. For once, I fear the worst. But my mind's made up. I'll go to London.

POLLY. Mercy save us! to London?

TOBY. To London; though I walk every inch of the way, and live upon blackberries. I'll see the young 'Squire himself.

POLLY. But why go,—why not write?

TOBY. No. A letter's but a scribbled bit of paper, to be tossed aside, and there an end. No! He shall look in my face and hear me talk. And if I don't bring the blood into his cheek, why, there's not a blush to be had from all London.

POLLY. Don't be rash. Do but consider who the 'Squire is, and who you are.

TOBY. That's what I intend to let him know. I shall tell him, if landlords are too proud or too idle to look after the comforts of their tenants, and to live upon their

own lands, why 'tis a great pity that Providence should
have entrusted them with any. What! haven't we paid
truly for sixty years? and now that a rascal should screw
and grind and crush us—No! 'tis a good thought, for it's
come so late.—I'll go to London.

POLLY. Martin may yet bring good news.

TOBY. He may; but I'll provide against the worst.
You go to Rachel. I'll be hence soon. My luggage
won't stop my speed upon the road. Yes, and now I
have it, I'll once more to the mansion; and if old Crumbs
be as deaf as ever, I'll see if the 'Squire himself be not
less hard of hearing than his servant.

Exit POLLY at side, and TOBY through door.

SCENE II.

A Copse.

Enter RACHEL in flight.

RACH. I hear his step. Yes, there again. 'Tis he.
Could I but gain the main road;—I cannot stir. I am
almost dead with grief and fear. (*She hides.*)

Enter SILVER JACK, in pursuit.

JACK. This was the place. I'm sure 'twas here!

Enter HYSSOP, hastily.

HYS. Jack, is't you?
JACK. Ay: did you pass a woman in fast flight?
HYS. A woman! Will you never be serious? Come
with me.
JACK. Stop till I have found my runaway.
HYS. And lost a golden prize. I was coming for you.
JACK. A prize!—What do you mean?

Hys. That visitor at the mansion! Why, he has heaps of guineas, rings, and a brilliant snuff-box, that alone would make us.

Jack. Well?

Hys. Well?—If you're the Silver Jack of yesterday they must be ours.

Jack. How?

Hys. Easily. He is now in bed. I have left open all the doors.—(*Rachel shows herself through the trees, listening.*) We can get into his chamber, and then——

Jack. But if he wake and resist?

Hys. A knife!

Jack. The booty is large?

Hys. I tell you enough to set us up.

Jack. Where the devil can that woman have flown?

Hys. A woman!—It's a pity women aren't thief-catchers, for they'd only have to show you the darbies, and you'd run your hands into 'em. Will you join me, or shall I do the work alone?

Jack. I'm for you. But you're too much of a philosopher; you should consider one's little frailties. (*taking out small pocket-pistols, and looking at priming, &c.*) Man was born to love, and that's my weakness. If he stir, here are two bullets for his head! The doors are open, you say?

Hys. Every one.——

Here Rachel expresses her resolution to give their victim notice, and glides off.

And now for the shiners.

Exeunt.

Enter MARTIN HEYWOOD.

MAR. Poor Rachel!—I hadn't the heart to go to the farm. For her—for my children's sake, I'll once more try to move the steward. It almost chokes me to think of it; but it must be tried. Every one refuses me: 'tis my last hope. If that fail too, 'tis needless to whimper about it,—good bye, farm !—good bye, England! I have promised to give my answer to-day: and it may be to-night we sleep upon the sea. Now for master Crumbs, to beg and pray, and be refused. He is an early riser, and I may now see him without fear of interruption. If he denies me, why then for a foreign home, for I have lost my own.

Exit.

SCENE III.

An old Gallery in the Mansion. Door in Scene, leading into Apartment.

Enter HYSSOP and JACK. RACHEL glides in, and retires at back.

HYS.   You see all the doors were open.

JACK.   Yes; it's what I call housebreaking made easy. No one stirring either.—Where's Crumbs?

HYS.   Vanished in a blue flame, for what I know. I hope he means no mischief; but I've scarcely seen him since he went with you to the farm.   Should he blow on us now?——

JACK.   He dares not; 'twould cost him his neck.

HYS.   Yet we'll not trust him.   We'll do this piece of work on our own behalf.   Then—for I've left nothing unprovided—there are a couple of horses, ready saddled, in the stable; we'll spare not the spur: and once off, let the steward settle the account as best he may.

JACK.   Where does the spark sleep?

HYS.   In yonder chamber. I have secured the key.

The bird is nicely caged. Come!—(*Goes to door; opens it, leaving the key in. Jack pulls Hyssop back.*)

JACK. Stay, Frank. I've been thinking of it:—there must be no blood in this.

HYS. That's at the option of the gentleman. I've no objection, if it can be made comfortable to him.

JACK. 'Twould make a stir that might be fatal to us. You must promise me.

HYS. As far as I can keep my temper I do. Now, then; for there's no time to lose. (*At this moment Rachel, who has secured the key, glides into the room. She is seen by Hyssop, who staggers back.*) Ha! trapped!

JACK. (*clapping his hand to his pistols.*) What do you mean?

HYS. A woman entered that room!

JACK. You dream! (*rushes to door and looks through key-hole.*)

HYS. (*listening.*) There! I hear her footstep.

JACK. Why, no! yes;—it is the farmer's wife!

HYS. And there! (*Rachel is heard to turn the key in the lock.*) She locks the door. We're rarely gulled. Now there's but one plan. We'll force the way.

JACK. (*stopping him and pointing off with astonishment.*) Her husband! (*they retire up.*)

Enter MARTIN.

MAR. All the doors open, yet not a soul about! (*sees them.*) Is the steward?—Surely (*recognizing Jack*) 'tis he who was put into the farm. (*aside.*)

JACK. (*to Hyssop.*) Peace! I have it.—You wanted the steward?

MAR. Yes. Did he not put you into my house?

H

JACK. Ay; but I've finished my errand there: 'twas not the pleasantest.

MAR. I come to beg for time. Had I any one to intercede for me——

JACK. You may be quite easy. You have a friend, depend on't.

MAR. I know not where.

JACK. (*Pointing to room.*) There! In that room is a young London spark, the 'Squire's acquaintance—the door locked, and with him,—yes, you'll keep the farm:—'twas he who sent me to your house.

MAR. He! for what?

JACK. You've a pretty wife, he has plenty of money.—I delivered my message, and there your wife is.

MAR. My wife! villain! (*seizes him.*) Unsay the slander—on your knees unsay it—or, were you the father of all lies, I would not quit you.

JACK. Leave your hold! I say your wife.

MAR. My Rachel! (*bewildered.*) Why, how you look at me!

JACK. Knock at the door, perhaps she'll answer.

MAR. I am a wretched, ruined man; but do not play with me. Grief has worn me, but revenge will make me strong. If this be a lie!—

JACK. Knock at the door.

MAR. There seems blood before my eyes; and I feel of a sudden weak and old.

JACK. Knock at the door.

MAR. I'll tear his life out!

HYS. Why, that's manful. Here's that will help you. (*cocking a pistol and forcing it into Martin's hand.*)

MAR. (*rushing to the door.*) Come out, I say!

Enter GRANTLEY, armed with a brace of pistols. RACHEL following him.

GRAN. (*speaking as he enters.*) Villains! I am armed!

MAR. Die!

RACH. (*screaming and running before Grantley.*) Martin! what would you?

MAR. What! you cling to him,—before my eyes!—Rachel Heywood, I forgive that man! (*dropping the pistol.—Jack and Hyssop glide off.*) Let him but send a bullet through the heart you've broken, and I will thank him with my last breath.

GRAN. This your husband,—and leagued with the robbers!

RACH. No, no; he knows not what he says. Grief has distracted him.

MAR. Yes, grief. Falsehood where I hoped for truth. Scorn, where I had looked for love. Shame, where I had built my greatest pride.

GRAN. Go, I pardon you—I spare you.

MAR. Pardon! Spare! I have at home four motherless children;—what! do you spare me them? Will you leave the poor man one miserable comfort?

RACH. Husband!

MAR. Can your lips yet say that word?—Heaven forgive you!—can you yet speak it? Let it be for the last time! Never let us look again upon each other's face. (*She clings to him.*) Away! (*casting her off.*) My heart sinks at your touch! I leave you; and may God pardon and protect you!

Rushes off.

RACH. Martin! Martin! Oh! he is lost with misery!

GRAN. Fear not: for your sake I will not accuse him.

RACH. Accuse!

GRAN. Nay, I perceive, and value your motives. You would not suffer your husband to become a criminal. You preserved, it may be, my life. I thank you and pardon him.

RACH. And was it for this I saved you?—for this have endured the bitterest words that wife can listen to?—for this have made him mad? Sir, I never saw you till this hour. I never heard of you till named by villains who would have destroyed you. Then I flew to give you warning— I saved you;—and you give me this reward,—suspicion of my husband.

GRAN. Your eloquence, my good woman, does not deceive me. The other villains shall be pursued. For your husband, trust me he is safe.

Exit.

RACH. 'Tis no matter.—I will go home. Home! did he not forbid me?—Oh! he knew not what he said. And yet he found me—Oh! that he should harbour such a thought! I will fly and explain all; for now I should go mad to live one moment from him.

Exit.

Enter CRUMBS.

CRUMBS. All is stored—all packed!—all the harvest of my thrift and enmity. Ye cursed walls, I leave ye to your owner,—to him whom I had vainly hoped to beggar

—to sink into the dust a wretched, undone spendthrift!—
May ye become the haunt of gamesters, — of hungry,
smooth-faced knaves, who flatter and devour! May ye be
staked upon a card, and pass from him who stakes ye!—
For ten years have I dwelt here, nursing my revenge. For
ten years has vengeance been to me as a food—a nourish-
ment. I have lived and gloated on it. May others finish
the ruin I've begun! Now I must leave, ere my visitor—
plagues light upon him!—be stirring. That villain, Jack,
is still at Heywood's farm,—his companion yet asleep. I
live within the gallows' foot whilst near them.—I have
hid my treasure in the laurel hedge.— I've bought the
captain of the vessel, and this night I leave the shore. I
walk 'mongst pitfalls whilst I tread it.

BULLFROG runs in.

BULL. Oh, master Crumbs! such an affair.

CRUMBS. Peace, ye roaring fool! (*going*)

BULL. Fool! Early as it is, you're the second man
who has called me a fool this morning. I come upon
business.

CRUMBS. To-night—to-morrow!

BULL. Not my maxim. Shut your door upon business, and business will soon forget to knock at it. Your
friend, Captain Jack,——

CRUMBS. What of him?

BULL. He might be a good hand to put in possession
if one were to distrain a nunnery; but where a quick eye
is to be kept on chairs and tables, he's as blind as Cupid.

CRUMBS. What jargon is this?

BULL. I only hope there'll not be an action; but, if
there should be,——

CRUMBS. Speak out, or I'll throttle you. *(grasping him.)*

BULL. There certainly is a conspiracy to call me fool and choke me. Don't stare at me in that manner: it isn't business-like

CRUMBS. Speak, or begone.

BULL. Well, then, it's a serious truth that the Heywoods might clear out the farm; for nobody is there to prevent them.

CRUMBS. Is that all!

BULL. All? what! where I have once seized? what's to become of my reputation? I employ nobody but respectable, steady men. The fact is, Captain Jack was above his calling; for he made love to the farmer's wife.

CRUMBS. Well!

BULL. Not well, Mr. Crumbs. When a man's on business, he should be above such trifles.

CRUMBS. Where is he now?

BULL. Run off—left the premises in the most scandalous manner. I shouldn't wonder if he comes here.

CRUMBS. *(aside)* I must begone.

BULL. You are not going? I must put another man in, you know? I say I must—

CRUMBS. Leave me.

BULL. Business! Who shall I put in? *(follows him.)*

CRUMBS. *(furiously.)* Any one—no one—the devil!

Rushes off.

BULL. I'll have nothing more to do with any of your acquaintance. Why, he's quite a fury. I see it: I know he dabbles;—stocks must have fallen. Nothing else could put a man in such a passion.

STEPHEN is hurrying across.

Stephen! Stephen!—I'll ask him.

STE. I can't stop now. The whole place is in an up-roar.

BULL. Well, they've kept it very quiet. What's the matter?

STE. There's been robbery, and nearly——

BULL. Robbery?

STE. Yes, and nearly murder.

BULL. Murder's very bad, but I hope there's no pro-perty lost?

STE. We don't know what's lost yet. But for the two chaps you drank with and were such friends, the gentle-man offers a reward for whoever seizes them.

BULL. A reward!—I'll put on my cricketing pumps and run directly. Are they thieves, think you?

STE. You've been more in their company than I have. There's Toby Heywood in the garden. Go and talk to him. Business, you know,——

BULL. Business!—right. Toby here! then I'll just run and put Nokes into the farm, and then after my friends. I say, what's happened to master Crumbs?

STE. Why, between you and me, the steward——but while I talk to you, I may miss what the gentleman offers.

Runs off.

BULL. Something wrong with the steward. If he should go out, I might come in. I'll run and show my activity.

Runs off.

SCENE IV.

The Interior of Heywood's Farm. Martin discovered, seated in his Arm Chair. His Children grouped about him.

MAR. And this, then, is the end! All's gone!—I cannot carry with me even a hope of better days. Now, indeed, labour will be hard to me; for I shall work with a broken heart. Now, fortune cannot bless me; for she with whom I should have shared all good——But let me think no more of her. Think no more! Like a ghost she seems to haunt me. But she has shamed me,—and may she——! No, I cannot curse her with her children looking in my face. I will not curse her. I must say farewell to the home where I was born—where I had hoped to die.—Oh! as I think of the long past days,—as I sit here staring my last at these walls,—those who are now in their graves come gathering about me:—faces, that seem a part of the place—that seem as they had never been away;—looks that take me back, and make me a child again.—All from then till now is like a dream;—the things of my boyhood alone seem real:—all else is——

RACH. (*without.*) Martin! Martin!

MAR. (*starting.*) No, no; that is real—would it were not! (*to children.*) Go, bolt the door.

BOY. Why, it is my mother. I mustn't bolt the door against my mother.

MAR. No.—I had forgot. A good child; you must not. (*The boy runs and opens the door.*)

RACH. (*running in.*) Martin! dear Martin!

MAR. (*rising.*) Rachel, if you can look in my face, and do not sink with shame, can you look on these?— (*pointing to children.*)

RACH. Shame!—you are deceived.

MAR. I have been: so deceived, that had a voice from the sky called you what it tears my heart to think of, I would not have listened to it. But these eyes—these eyes!—oh! that I had been blind!

RACH. You never loved me if you will not hear me.

MAR. Never loved you! It was that love that smoothed all trouble to me. It was that love, that, when all men,—fortune,—seemed set against me, cheered me on, and put a strength into my heart,—that made me smile as I would think—Well, let all go, let all else fail me, there is one who'll never change;—there is one who is as good, as constant as the angels. Poverty came upon me: the blow was sudden and unkind. Still I thought, though we have but a crust, we'll share that crust together; though our bed be straw, that bed shall bear us both!—As you say, I am deceived.

RACH. But hear me, Martin; then judge me as you will!

MAR. That man—that devil, whom they put here— would his blood were on my hearth!—did he not tempt you?

RACH. He did.—

MAR. With gold—filthy gold?—He came into the poor man's house—bought that which I thought worlds could never buy—robbed me of my wife, these children of their mother.

RACH. Martin, may you be pardoned that thought!—It is true that man showed me gold—dared to speak—to seize me,—but I cast his money in the dust, I tore myself from his arms.—

MAR. His arms! (*passionately.*) Woman! I would not kill you.

RACH. I fled and hid myself—listened to a plan of murder, and ran to the mansion.—

MAR. I found you there, coming from his chamber.

RACH. I knew not the man! 'Twas to save his life. Upon my soul I speak the truth!

MAR. (*with emotion.*) A lie—a foul lie!

RACH. The truth, or may I die at your feet. Oh, Martin! can you think thus of me,—after the years—the happy years?—Or am I become tiresome to you, and so with this excuse you'd——

MAR. Excuse! Are these tears an excuse,—these trembling limbs, these scalded eyes, this broken heart? (*Sinks into chair.*)

Enter Sailor.

SAILOR. (*speaking at door.*) Now, master, if you're for starting, we shall sail in an hour. Here's a whole crew of neighbours, too, coming to take leave of you.— (*disappears from door.*)

RACH. Martin!

MAR. I have accepted the place abroad, to tend an

estate, (*with suppressed disgust.*) and overlook the slaves. I leave the farm—the country, this day.

RACH. The children?—

MAR. They go with me.

RACH. And I, Martin—I?

MAR. Go where you will, may you be happy.

RACH. (*wildly.*) My children! Use me as you please, —but my babes!—Oh, Martin! what madness is upon you? Hear me! You shall hear me. If it must be so, think not of me as your wife; but have mercy on the mother of your children!

MAR. I love them, Rachel.

RACH. Dearly, very dearly; but not like a mother.

MAR. Bid them farewell, for they must go.

RACH. But not without me! Children, pray to your father—pray to him I must not call my husband! (*Kneeling to Martin.*)

MAR. Rachel, this is wild and useless. Be calm and give them up.

RACH. I tell you I shall go mad—raving mad—to lose my children! Take me with them. I do not ask you to speak to me, to look at me;—let me work with the slaves you speak of;—let me die, so as I die not from my children! (*Faints, and falls over the knee of Martin—the children surrounding her.*)

Enter Farmer BEANSTALK, POLLY, DAME, NEIGHBOURS, and SAILOR.

FARMER. Why, Martin, and bee'st thee really going? (*sees Rachel.*) Why, what's the matter with thee wife?

POLLY. Bless me, Rachel! (*They bear her to the back.*)

MAR. Farmer, farewell; neighbours, heaven bless you!—Let the landlord take all the rest,—this chair,— my grandfather's chair,—I'll bear with me.

Enter BULLFROG *and two rustics at door.*

BULL. Not a splinter of it, as I'm a sworn appraiser.

MAR. I do not wish to hurt you, man; but do not strive to prevent me.

BULL. Mustn't move a stick, Mr. Heywood. Business is business.

MAR. I tell you this chair shall with me. Let him who dares, lay a finger on it. (*Is about to lift the chair: Bullfrog advances.*)

BULL. Business is business. I seize in the king's name!

MAR. Then you must fight for it. (*Strikes Bullfrog, who seizes the chair with the rustics. The neighbours assist Martin, exclaiming, "Down with them!" In the struggle, the back of the chair is pulled off, when out fall loose gold, small money-bags and a paper.*)

ALL. Gold! Money!

BULL. I seize it in the king's name.

FARMER. (*throwing him aside.*) What be this? (*taking up paper.*) Your grandfather's name.

MAR. (*Takes paper, glances at it, endeavouring to read it, and then returns it to Beanstalk.*) Read, read!

FARMER. (*reads.*) " *Should any sudden accident light upon me, so that I be not able to tell my last wishes, let this certify, that the three hundred guineas hidden, with this paper, in my walnut chair, be the rightful property of Martin and Tobias Heywood, my grandsons. Signed,*

Thomas Heywood." This is rare, Martin! I give thee joy! (*Neighbours shout.*)

MAR. I shall keep the farm!—ha! ha!—I shall keep the farm! (*sinks upon the neck of farmer.*)

Enter GRANTLEY at Door.

GRAN. Where is master Heywood?

MAR. Come not here, man—come not here!

GRAN. Be calm. I have injured you—in thought, I mean. All your neighbours praise you for an honest, upright man. I thought you the companion of scoundrels. But for your wife, whose devotedness I have wronged, I had fallen their victim. She came to save me——

TOBY, without.

Come along, rascal. Stand out of the way!

Enters, dragging in CRUMBS. SERVANT following, carrying a box.

CRUMBS. Villain! why am I thus used?

TOBY. (*to Grantley.*) Here is the rascal, sir. You know we found that box among the laurel trees. Luckily, you took my advice, and let it rest. We watched, and, as I expected, the thief came creeping down to carry away the spoil. We pounced upon him,—here he is, and here's his plunder.

GRAN. What answer make you to this?

CRUMBS. None to you. I shall make a clear answer to Mr. Robert Grantley.

GRAN. Then speak. Robert Grantley is before you.

(*general surprize.*) What! you shrink?—I had heard of your oppression. I wrote for further sums of money, and then, under a feigned character, came to witness the means you'd take to answer the demand. Fie upon you! My father left you to husband my estate; it was your duty to check my extravagance, not feed it. And now, you add to your iniquity by wholesale theft. What say you to this?

CRUMBS. Robert Grantley,—since you are he,—listen. At the mansion you saw a certain picture. You remember you asked me whose it was? I'll tell you. It was the likeness of a young and once virtuous wife. A devil, a golden devil, dazzled her vain heart, and she left her husband and disgraced him. That husband plunged in vice to fly from thought. He gamed, robbed, and was devoted to the thief's reward—the gallows. He escaped, and fled abroad. Years passed away. In a foreign land he met his wife's destroyer, who, knowing not the man he had wronged, fostered him—took him to his heart—made him his man of trust, and brought him to England. He died, and left him to manage his estate for his wild and absent son. Robert Grantley, that man was your father; the picture is the picture of his victim; I—I was her wronged and broken-hearted husband!

GRAN. Can it be?

CRUMBS. My purpose was to beggar you—to revenge me on the father, in his dearest part, his darling son!

GRAN. Your injuries were great; yet how could your malice survive the author of your wrongs?

CRUMBS. That picture! I have stood and looked at it, —in the still night I have gazed on it, until I have thought the devil himself looked from its eyes, and smiled upon my purpose. That picture, and the recollection that those cursed walls received my wife when she fled from her home, and left me to seek companions with the vile and infamous—Oh! I am an old man!—but there are injuries so graven in the heart, so burnt within the brain, that with the heart and brain must live and die together! Enough. Now for my gaol.

GRAN. No; I pardon you: nay, more; will provide for you.

CRUMBS. Never. I scorn and spit at you.—Am I free?

STEPHEN and others bring in SILVER JACK and HYSSOP, bound.

STE. Here are the thieves! (to Grantley.) I was told you were here, sir, and so here I've brought them.— Bob, the carter here, saw them on the road, and, knowing our cattle, gave the cry; they were soon unhorsed, and here they are, ready trussed for the gibbet. We found these few matters on them. (showing dice, cards, picklocks, &c.) And here's something folded up. (gives paper to Grantley.)

GRAN. What is this?—(reading bill) "Escaped from Newgate—John Harris!"—Who can this mean?

CRUMBS. The man your father robbed! Read, and see what time and he have made of him. I took ten guineas from a rich usurer, and was condemned for Tyburn. Your father stole the wife of my bosom, and lived a wealthy, charitable gentleman,—had the respect of all while on the earth, and a lying tombstone when under it! May I leave now? (Grantley bows.)

CRUMBS looks fiercely around him, exchanges a look of contempt with JACK and HYSSOP, and rushes off.

JACK. Perhaps we're intruding: may we leave too?

GRAN. Away with them, and keep them for the present.

STE. They deserve hanging if it's only for the lies they told about master Heywood's wife. Why, they've been laughing over it as a good joke,—(*Jack and Hyssop laugh,*)—that they tried to make Martin jealous, that he might save them the sin of blowing out your brains. Oh! you rascals!—your hanging-day will be a rare holiday thirty miles round.

STEPHEN, &c. take JACK and HYSSOP off.

MAR. Rachel! can I be forgiven? I dare not look at you. (*Rachel throws herself into his arms.*)

TOBY. I don't wonder at that. He's a poor wizard whom every fool can drive mad. Suspect Rachel! why, if we weren't all made so happy with our grandfather's gold, I'd turn boy again, and thrash you myself. Here was Bullfrog trying to disturb me and my wife.

BULL. Wife!

TOBY. Yes. I shall never know what to do with my part of the money, so I must have a wife, to get her advice about it. (*Taking Polly's arm.*) I hope (*to Bull.*) you've no objection?

BULL. None, (*aside.*) as the money's not on the other side. But business is business; you'll want furniture: I have the sweetest four-post bedstead you ever looked upon.

MAR. (*to Gran.*) I have now, sir, to ask your pardon. Can you excuse the passion of an oppressed——

GRAN. Nay, it is I who have to ask forgiveness of you, and of all my tenants; that I have suffered them to be the victims of a mercenary agent. I will, henceforth, reside on my lands; and, by my future care, endeavour to remedy the injuries committed by my servant. To your wife, Heywood, I probably owe my existence. This farm has, I hear, been in your family for sixty years: may it remain so while the country stands! To-morrow shall give you a freeholder's right to it.

NEIGHBOURS, &c. Huzza! Huzza!

BULL. Well, this is capital. I see (*aside.*) I'm future steward to that young man. But still I have to say one thing. Friendship and generosity are very well; but— (*to Martin.*) now, it doesn't concern you,—you're a freeholder: all of us here aren't so lucky: therefore, as business is business, I trust nobody here will forget

"THE RENT DAY."

THE END.

K

Printed by LOWE and HARVEY, Playhouse-yard, Blackfriars.

Dramatic Works published by C. CHAPPLE, Royal Library, Pall Mall.

TRAGEDIES.

ABRADATAS and PANTHEA; a Tragedy, from the Cyropædia of Xenophon. By *John Edwards, Esq.* of Old Court, near Dublin, 8vo., price 2s. 6d.

BOHEMIAN; a Tragedy, in Five Acts, by *George Soane, A.B.*, 8vo. price 4s. 6d.

BONDUCA; a Tragedy, from Beaumont and Fletcher, by *George Colman, Esq.* price 2s. 6d.

PHILOSOPHER; a Tragedy, in Five Acts, from the German of Lessing, by *H. M. Milner,* price 2s. 6d.

PLEDGE; or, Castilian Honour: a Tragic Drama, in Five Acts, by *James Kenney, Esq.* 8vo. price 3s.

PIZARRO in PERU; or, the Death of Rolla: by *Thomas Dutton,* 8vo. price 2s. 6d.

ROLLA; or, the Peruvian Hero: a Tragedy, in Five Acts, by *M. G. Lewis, Esq.* 8vo. price 2s. 6d.

SEDUCER; a Tragedy, in Five Acts, by *Charles Masterton, Esq.* 8vo. price 2s. 6d.

COMEDIES.

GOLDEN GLOVE; or, the Farmer's Son: a Comedy, in Five Acts, by *John Lake,* 8vo. price 3s. 6d.

MY WIFE or MY PLACE; a Petite Comedy, in Two Acts, by *Charles Shannon* and *Thomas William Thackeray,* 8vo. price 2s. 6d.

MY WIFE! WHAT WIFE? a Comedy, in Three Acts, by *Eaton Stannard Barrett, Esq.* 8vo. price 2s. 6d.

SCHOOL FOR FRIENDS; a Comedy, in Five Acts, by *Miss Chambers,* 8vo. price 2s. 6d.

STUDENTS OF SALAMANCA; or, The Delusion: a Comedy, in Five Acts, by *Robert Francis Jameson, Esq.* 8vo. price 3s.

TOUCH AT THE TIMES; a Comedy, in Five Acts, as performed at the Theatre Royal Covent Garden, by *Robert Francis Jameson, Esq.* of the Inner Temple, price 2s. 6d.

TOUCHSTONE; or, The World as it Goes: a Comedy, in Four Acts, by *James Kenney,* 8vo. price 3s.

COMIC OPERAS.

ABROAD AND AT HOME; a Comic Opera, in Three Acts, by *J. G. Holman,* 8vo. price 3s. 6d.

BARBER OF SEVILLE; a Comic Opera, in Two Acts, as performed at the Theatre Royal Covent Garden. The Overture and Music entirely new. Composed by *Bishop.* 8vo. price 2s.

TWO FACES UNDER A HOOD; a Comic Opera, in Three Acts, by *Thomas Dibdin,* 8vo. price 2s. 6d.

VIRGIN OF THE SUN; an Operatic Drama, by *Frederick Reynolds,* fourth edition, 8vo. price 2s. 6d.

VETERAN; or, the Farmer's Sons: a Comic Opera, in Five Acts, by *E. P. Knight,* 8vo. price 2s. 6d.

PLAYS.

ACCUSATION; or, the Family of D'Anglade: a Play, in Three Acts, by *John Howard Payne,* 8vo. price 2s. 6d.

COURAGE REWARDED; or, The English Volunteer: a Political Drama, in Three Acts, 8vo. price 1s. 6d.

HOUSE OF MORVILLE; or, Disinherited Son: a Drama, in Five Acts, by *John Lake.* With a brief Sketch of the Author's Life, by the late *James Grant Raymond,* price 3s.

LOOK AT HOME; a Play, in Three Acts, by the late *E. I. Eyre*. Second Edition, 8vo. price 2s. 6d.

RENEGADE; a grand Historical Drama, in Three Acts, by *Frederick Reynolds*, 8vo. price 2s. 6d.

TIMON OF ATHENS; altered from Shakspeare, by the *Hon. George Lamb*, 8vo. price 2s. 6d.

WANDERER; or, The Rights of Hospitality: a Drama, in Three Acts, by *Charles Kemble*, 8vo. price 2s. 6d.

MELO-DRAMAS.

EDDA; or, The Hermit of Warkworth: a Melo-drama, in Two Acts, by *Edward Ball*, price 2s.

MILLER AND HIS MEN; a Melo-drama, in Two Acts, by *Isaac Pocock*. A new Edition, 8vo. price 2s.

PEASANT OF LUCERN; a Melo-drama, in Three Acts, by *George Soane, A.B.* 8vo. price 3s. 6d.

RUGANTINO; or, The Bravo of Venice: a grand Romantic Melo-drama, by *M. G. Lewis, Esq.* 8vo. price 2s. 6d.

FARCES.

ALL IN THE DARK; or, The Banks of the Elbe: a Musical Farce, in Two Acts, by *J. R. Planche*, 8vo. price 2s. 6d.

ANTIQUITY, a Farce, in Two Acts, by *Barron Field, Esq.* 8vo. 2s.

AT HOME; a Farce, with Music, in Two Acts, by the *Rev. Sir Henry Bate Dudley, Bart.* 8vo. price 2s.

BOARDING HOUSE; or, Five Hours at Brighton; a Musical Farce, in Two Acts, by *Samuel Beazley, Jun.* Fourth Edition, 8vo. price 2s.

CHIP OF THE OLD BLOCK; or, The Village Festival: a Musical Farce, in Two Acts, by *E. P. Knight*, Comedian, 8vo. price 2s.

CROTCHET LODGE; a Farce, (with New Songs by the Author), in Two Acts, by *Thomas Hurlestone*, Fourth Edition, 8vo. price 2s.

DARKNESS VISIBLE; a Farce, in Two Acts, by *Theodore Edward Hook, Esq.* Third Edition, 8vo. price 2s.

DAY AFTER THE WEDDING. By *Mrs. C. Kemble*. Second Edition, 8vo. price 2s.

FAIR GABRIELLE; an Operatic Anecdote, in One Act. By *J. R. Planche*, 8vo. price 2s.

HOUSE OUT AT WINDOWS. A Musical Piece, in Three Acts, by *James Kenney*, 8vo. price 2s.

HOW TO DIE FOR LOVE; a Farce, in Two Acts, by the *Baron Langsdorff*. Fourth Edition, 8vo. price 2s.

KILLING NO MURDER; a Farce, in Two Acts, by *Theodore Edward Hook, Esq.* 8vo. price 2s.

LOTTERY TICKET, or the Lawyer's Clerk, a Farce, in One Act, by *Sam. Beazley*, 8vo. price 2s.

LADIES AT HOME; or Gentlemen we can do without you; a Farce, in One Act, by the Author of the Bee-hive, 8vo. price 1s. 6d.

MUSIC MAD, a Dramatic Sketch, by *Theodore Edward Hook, Esq.* 8vo. price 2s.

MAN IN THE MOON; a Farce, in Two Acts, by *R. Phillips*, of the Theatre Royal Drury Lane, 8vo. price 2s.

NONDESCRIPT; a Musical Farce, in Two Acts, 8vo. price 2s. 6d.

PLOT AND COUNTERPLOT; or the Portrait of Michael Cervantes; a Farce, by *Charles Kemble*. Second Edition, 8vo. price 2s.

REFORMATION; a Comic Interlude, by *J. B. Pulham*, 8vo. 1s. 6d.

SHARP AND FLAT; a Musical Farce, by *Denis Lawler*, 8vo. 2s.

SLEEP WALKER; a Farce, in Two Acts, by *W. C. Oulton*. 8vo. 2s.

WEST WIND; or Off for London; a Farce, in Two Acts, by *Wm. Wastell, Esq.* 8vo. price 2s.

Lightning Source UK Ltd.
Milton Keynes UK
UKOW02f1940091013

218792UK00008B/717/P